Earth from the Moon

Also by Judith E.P. Johnson

Mountain Moods (VDL Publications, 1997)

Gatherers (VDL Publications, 1998)

Fragments (VDL Publications, 2000)

Selected Poems CD (7 RPH, 2001)

Snapshot (Regal Press, 2003)

Landmarks (Ginninderra Press, 2005)

Alone at the Window (Ginninderra Press, 2012)

Between Two Moons (Ginninderra Press, 2015)

Waking from Dreams (Ginninderra Press, 2016)

Where It Leads (Ginninderra Press, 2018)

Only the Waves (Ginninderra Press, 2019)

Briefly in Spring (Ginninderra Press, 2020)

Day Moon Fading (Ginninderra Press, 2021)

Judith E.P. Johnson

Earth from the Moon

haiku & senryu

Acknowledgements

The author has had many haiku presented in journals, on radio, and online. The haiku in *Earth from the Moon* are new and unpublished, except for those which appeared in *Milestones, I Protest!, Echidna Tracks, Windfall* and *Ko*.

Special thanks are due to Peter Macrow for his kindness and inspiration, to my children Karen, Debra and Craig for their encouragement and support, to Jane Williams for editing this book, and to Katherine Johnson for the cover design.

Earth from the Moon: haiku & senryu
ISBN 978 1 76109 360 9
Copyright © text Judith E.P. Johnson 2022
Cover: Katherine Johnson

First published 2022 by
Ginninderra Press
PO Box 3461 Port Adelaide SA 5015
www.ginninderrapress.com.au

for Graeme

milestone
another flaming arrow
misses me

sunlit window
in a dressing table mirror
bird flying

long letter
there's more
between the lines

new generation
in the family tree
great-grandmother greater

warm breeze
a whiff of blossoms
and house paint

apricot gold
its secret sealed
in a stone

meadow honey
I close my eyes
on clover and buttercups

I wait for a clock hour
to pass
timeless in space

this moment we share
tomorrow
the memory

bush birdsong
a sudden silence
log lorry passing

protest platform
the twelve-foot wide
tree stump

old friend
every day there for me
giant eucalypt

outdoor café
round the table
we follow the shade

back home
a spider's thread
attaches my chair to the wall

autumn rainbow
in a handbasket
garden fruit

rain and shine
all my life
dancing with you

so tiny
this seed I plant
almost not there

Earthbound
I watch
the stars singing

goldfish pond
visible through sunlit weeds
the plug

hole in the fence
child peeks
at another world

moon-white
vanishing into darkness
a bush moth

after choir
talking with friends
her musical laughter

busy street
everyone
in a dream world

outdoor pot plants
a sun shower
from the watering can

remote midden
only a flock of gulls
circling

now you have gone
your life story
in those left behind

creation myth
so many
buried in language

wrecked on rocks
a ship
in a bottle

out of its world
into my world
beach cuttlefish

hot sun
under the hedge
a breeze and I linger

flashing
high in gum leaves
the midday sun

wild garden
her neighbour's children
hiding

bowl of shells
last year's holiday
so long ago

footprints
criss-crossing a dusty track
traces of moonlight

sun rising
nightmares
fall behind me

unknowable
the heavens
and the mustard seed

letter
the warm glow
of your company

glass case cabochons
sunset agate
and pale moonstone

free range
a hen's egg
in my neighbour's flower pot

watching monkeys
shrieking and jumping
the children

rivulet
a platypus ripples
the sky

the toddler's face
in kitchen drawer knobs
upside down

nightfall
the mountain reveals
a new moon

wearing sunglasses
a child
toasts marshmallows

house for sale
empty rooms fill
with echoes

from beyond the mist
call
of the forest raven

ploughed paddock
petrified wood
and stone tools

stepping stone path
a child
jumps over flowers

poised heaven high
an eagle's shadow
on the earth

leaf, shell, feather
her sketch
a poem

dog beach
the husky finds
another husky

children's laughter
murmur
of the incoming tide

full moon…
in the river
in my cup

pre-dawn
out of darkness
the landscape changing

cold kitchen
the warm sound
of porridge

roosters
at rooster corner
homeless

high winds
a sudden shadow
covers the garden

zero degree
the warm hug
of my woollen jacket

carefully packaged
memories
in cellar cobwebs

in and out
waves sluicing the sands
of memory

words fail
we sit and hold hands
into the night

forever
this moment
achasing the wind

from leafy shrubs
the call
of perfumed flowers

rising sun
gravity keeps
my feet on the ground

daffodils
across the path
their long shadows

Sunday afternoon tea
the smell
of mown grass

exchanging glances
without a word
the kiss

fiddling with this
fiddling with that
a day passes

appearing in darkness
where from
this world of dreams

all my years
round and round I go
with the earth

between office blocks
a wispy cloud
on the mountain

deserted
a child's sandpit
noisy with sparrows

my home
the world
my nest

how blue her eyes
her dress
the world at her feet

gritty tin shut
on shells
cry of gulls and the sea

a full orchestra
playing softly
my kitchen radio

lights out
in bed
the day comes back

strange dream
I tell it in images
I know

soft light aglow
in golden leaves
the dying day

everywhere
aflame in grey bush
the waratah

left alone
the ancient forest
still there

coffee table
in a picture book
extinct animals

compressed
under city buildings
the living earth

giant digger
every day
small boy says hello

lunar light
shining on the lawn
the dew appears

dining alone
I light a candle
for company

faces fading
names unknown
Brownie box snapshot

noisy café
in a corner
man reading

cupboard cleaned
the skeleton gone
its story told

handle with care
the words
on the tip of your tongue

eclipse
our shadow
puts out the moon

old garden
waiting for the child
snapdragons

deserted cottage
carved in stone
the broad arrow

rose garden
far from home
a honey bee

day by day
suddenly
the end of the road

misunderstood
only music understands
heartache

home again
stepping off the plane
into mountain air

snug in my chair
stories
of survival

worst and best
in later years
time alone

mountain trail
taking time
for the little flowers

walking track
following the river
old coach road

always there
the seaside shack
of family dreams

snowflake by snowflake
the garden path
whitens

balancing
a butterfly
grips my finger

young guelder rose
soft on my palm
the first snowball

holding the earth
clearing the air
the old forest

universe
alone
I am the centre

ferryboat
drifting offshore
a scent of islands

motionless
in falling leaves
the rusty swing

baby sparrows
twig to twig
overgrown hedge

over the hills
disappearing
road without end

blue flash
across the tannin river
kingfisher

child's knitted gloves
a face smiling
on each finger

two young dogs on a lead
in a pusher
the old dog

spring sunshine
I check gardening gloves
for spiders

in my sleep mother says
with language
you can redeem your dreams

downpour
after the concert
louder than applause

empty room
a guitar string twangs
midnight freeze

morning frost
granddaughter wears
honeybee earrings

wisteria
its blue perfume
I wish I could show you

a flower from each plant
in the vase
her garden

homegrown
mother's lavender bag
childhood fresh

dawn sky
in a dry creek bed
nocturnal footprints

sun sinking
children in the shallows
won't come

wildlife park
hello!
calls a white cockatoo

humming
a bee disappears
into a pink hibiscus

call of the mopoke
through dark trees
wallaby thudding

old friend
where are you
now spring is here?

long slow day
iced drinks
and Miles Davis

now you have gone
who will remember
my childhood?

leaves flying
park trees
naked in the wind

mountain café
in morning mist
the fairy wrens

first light
on the white mountain
untrodden snow

precious photo
earth from the moon
my home

www.ingramcontent.com/pod-product-compliance
Lightning Source LLC
Chambersburg PA
CBHW070337120526
44590CB00017B/2924